FRØZEN
ACCIDENT

FRØZEN ACCIDENT

BY

Alfred
Arteaga

TIA CHUCHA PRESS
LOS ANGELES

PARA
RUBI OROZCO

Printed in the United States of America

ISBN 1-882688-32-5

Book Design: Jane Brunette
Cover Photo: *L.A. Familia 2*. Pictured: Victor Carrillo. ©2004, Harry Gamboa Jr.

PUBLISHED BY:
Tia Chucha Press
A Project of Tia Chucha's Centro Cultural
PO Box 328
San Fernando, CA 91341
www.tiachucha.com

DISTRIBUTED BY:
Northwestern University Press
Chicago Distribution Center
11030 South Langley Avenue
Chicago, IL 60628

Tia Chucha Press is supported by the National Endowment for the Arts and operating funds from Tia Chucha's Centro Cultural. Tia Chucha's Café & Centro Cultural have received support from the Los Angeles Department of Cultural Affairs, the Center for Cultural Innovation, the Middleton Foundation, Not Just Us Foundation, the Liberty Hill Foundation, Youth Can Service, Toyota Sales, Solidago Foundation, and other grants and donors including Bruce Springsteen, John Densmore, Dan Attias, Dave Marsh, Suzan Erem, Cynthia Cuza, Mel Gilman, Tony & Jennie LoRe, Denise Chávez and John Randall of the Border Book Festival, and Luis & Trini Rodríguez.

contents

3/3: CALIFORNIA NO ES ISLA

1/3:

derrida and wittgenstein

1   Frozen-like Accident

"yet," you say zero
more of ciphers
the font being 2 full

figures mark
how natural sign bleeds
colors tear spread loose
zero by drop 1
"finger was stained"
like virgin image
how rhythm of cold water
becomes areola light
and again

2　Red Zero

yellow more "red"
than extreme
absent the
math

of color
blood gradient, an
arc flesh flushed
hunger rings from night
perhaps "deictic wine marks"
and seemless gradient
conform to spill
across long wave
pure, blind
and spirit

3   One Extreme

You envision "hair"
breadths of moment
before the rest
and consonance of
dihydrous oxide

which "could be ink"
if color were
graded tears but
no, nothing never
happens first, 4
its not really it
till its accounted 4

4 New Euros

Change "persists
in" this French
etymology erase
the point
erase the prior

point "directed"
from an image wholly
fair before
1's own eros

5   Final Exit

"Memory" tracks
the train
thought to reach
the German terminal

"away & out"
distant vision distant
phonic and scope
each falls back
upon its only course

the sign exit
exit and sortie
nullified
sortie and exit
excited corpse

6 EndZ1

the letters B through Y
"mere hemoglobin"
river between font
faded A, source A,
and no exit Z,
sortie teleology
perspective
perfect

 "from icon red"
vanishing beyond
infraredolent point
A, beyond ultraviolent
point B, facing
Xclusive distance

7   Schema

"synaptic rust" is itself
trust pathos causeway,
incidental fax and
fixed set of wound,
is history

is rapture
"originals in" matters
given to procreate
in his image
know history
so it can be repeated

8   Mist

Simply put is
"radiant where"
seeming rays radiate
and body temperature
phonemes reach
4 more zero
yet reach
but reaching

"heat and" motion
expiate nothing
pointed 2 surpasses
reception
reflection
or refraction
pointing to all
misses nothing

9 Areola

The imagined
"finger was stained"
glass, the eye scene
a mirror, cold water
marks syntactile skin
terminates any out
of line work

"yet" a paraphrase
gained, tense taut
and stable for life
1 clean parallel:
a distant lost rapture
not quite first
a last stop final destination
X itself

2/3:

nezahualcoyotl
in mictlan

10 Red

Field

Take the interior of zero
soft fleshy palpable
no, an interior from which
to radiate original syntheses,

cardinal points the navel
of locus, one circle around
the topos of field and grid
complete geometries, and the slight

slight curve of calculus,
1 whole zero offering up
proof of god in its fact
between water and between the waters

a red sky, blackish, blacker
long degrees 122
and yellow, pale, toward white
white, 37 levels,

white, the peninsula of St. Francis
a plate of peace, one cape,
the birth of island, more yellow
still, there, 1 red, more absent,

blacker, across 1 yellow breeding
presence, broken brilliant
blank after blank: 1 whole
zero, catholic its immaculate

cipher, first synthesis, origin
of encircled sign completes
the ring of god and some
San Francisco May day

primavera of the cross, of those
colors: the north and west axis
of the absent presence, white
and across, black, the east

This Point of Hours

ern sky is red, blushed rage
across black aiming long
waves toward none, a rage of
music given body in the reach

of light, the mountain range
the bay, the long river, the foothills,
it is life spilled, seens
of painted life alive

there in the color break,
San Francisco meridian May
pimavera, life as in alife:
the air hard blue,

fog parts fold to bay,
a keen edged daylight strikes
glare, incises clean against
blue, pieces of painted

lives commence color,
the sound of metal strain, the
spikes of brain activity and
the polylogue of tint, tone and

shade, there, the convergence of
levels, acts and cardinals,
exactly radiant, pointing to all
not absent like conjoined heavy air

and light bent through water,
born there ocean bay and
urine, the junction of thing,
facts image beyond the

capacity of inks, the red
and black, to imagine life in
center, whole and complete,
inside the cipher the origin

alias but not really, know
ledge at the tip of peninsularity
is only half Euro terminus,
only half capital terminate,

only half endzone cochineal:
Wartezeit für mich, bitte

Freezing Point

The point is plain: a unitary
identity less hole than field
of flags, colors flat
on cardinal grid less

solitary than ratio of axes.
than right lengths at right widths,
where it acts an episteme
and facts apparent, joy

in the shape of human surface,
a machine transforms energy,
a field of organic intellectual,
a collection of items from youth,

a busy intersection, a museum
near the metro, a red bridge
blind to ocean, and the people
you've known. The point thus given

body there, May day primavera,
everything pointed to in arcs
from efulgent core each ray
illuminates some trace fact

scene there, the point not one
but zero corporeal irradiates
from there, each present pointed to,
in a sense named, even if ignored,

all and every shined upon,
around corners, in dream, in long waves
of light eros quiver.
There are the points: San Francisco,

a glass of water, a digit stained.

11 Yellow

Blood Site

I, Nezahualcoyotl, poet of Texcoco,
born in the year 1-Rabbit,
son of Ixtlilxochitl and of Matlalcihuatzin,
grandson of Huitzilihuitl the Mexica,

in 4-Rabbit, my sixteenth year,
have seen the yellow earth
home, bright dirt, the bright sky,
bright flower of yellow Texcoco,

cover in red, the deep red
changing black, the color
of my father's blood, in his blood
let from his incise flesh, the red

zero of his life zero
at the hand, in acts of assassins,
men and night edge flint
blood tracks, until my father

changed to body only flesh,
a trail of cipher red,
before the near and beside,:
dead Ixtlilxochitl, father mine,

voice and spirit of Texcoco,
I have seen you die.

Canto of Flight

Flowers wither and sound
brittle things break, floral
cries pitch rage
again in short wave

and out, an image venadita:
one small deer painted
cripple, each small leg
pierced eros such anima,

such gesture could come to pass
2: black orchids and the small
red mammal fade
from sense, wither and dry

blood spurts, and the grave
tremors disappear from site,
¿adónde van los desaparecidos?
Only in song am I answered
only in song may I see them
still, bright flower
and singing painted deer
cross river points,

en el agua y en los matorrales.
Equis, the tlahcuiloco, acts,
gives lyric, presence to the fall
of father, to the fall of mother deer,

presence to the hummingbird past,
the lyric petals beating
like hooves brings life again
before me those as if alive,

Equis, Tochihuitzin Coyolchiuhqui,
gives pitch to the red and to the black,
the inks that draw life
from the dead, gives rhythm

to the flight of green birds
in lyric of absence somehow full
and complete, pregnant, flush,
his lyrics tear my home past,

make me change, take flight, leave
the home of souls who stood
beside me and will never be,

song of flight: Run cholo run,
to the island causeways impermanent,
flee to the island hummingbird,
to cactus, from yellow home

made red, changed black, go
to an island half mine, become
the cipher painted in inks
over yellow. BB = 2 flee.

Motion

Heart beat is never twice
river, the image font
a dream wood of liquid
form in the site of dead

souls, the lyrics follow blood
points, life edge words
shape to melody, to beat

of heart like flight of the small.
I am not the man who was.
I, Nezahualcoyotl, take
flight in the graphite river,

change place for life,
leave for an island and beyond.
Run cholo run, flee
the red reach and night.

12   Black

In Xochitl In Cuicatl

Lyric points me to the end
of green, where yellow earth
holds stem and petal all hours,
where yellow and green transform

clean to blue and to fluid
wave of earth and sky,
the lyric points away
from yellow Texcoco Xopan,

to an island cross blue,
only in lyric lies
this meaning, the only truths
in fluid: true, the world fades,

blackens where blood springs
and opens where I must face
truly, an island half mine
and there find way beyond,

 to the place of flags, a pale dog,
last stop for meaning, to Mictlan,
realm of dead souls, laws,
stories where meanings reside.

Isla Negra

I face the night before me
as sung in floricanto and seen
in perfect inks: I strain
in the clean night zero

to see an island amid waves
of black water, an image, a man
comes to view and as space
halves, one man, one boat.

Gato takes shape before me,
speaks: I will change your home,
board the boat, for ahead
lie the night and island, half home,

final exit for the dead. His words
faint songs, his motions precise,
we board the boat and he pushes off
silent, effortless, we glide

over black ripples, before us
island and black city etch
cold against night sky,
the waters beneath us strewn

here and again with petals,
orchids and magnolia, the water
churns and moans low as we cross,
sad moans and those of dolor,

as if petals were faces watching
my flight. We strikes earth
and debark to black earth and sky.
Gato leaves and I follow

to city wall, to portal, we enter
the night city's narrow passages,
men and women there sit
on silent stone, faces

buried in hands, silent
or weakly shaking, eyes closed,
so much the incarnation of moaning
petals, no one sees

us across the night to the point
where Gato fades beside
the distant portal and disappears
amid the night soul.

Causeway

The far portal points from the city
away and out to the night
sky, dark trees and island end
there at black waters edge,

there one figure in absent light,
lone woman in black huipil,
her long hair darkest burgundy
integral to this night of hours,

she motions me come to her,
I try to speak but she fills
the air with words in tones
sure as they are sad: I will take you

to Mictlan, we will cross the sad
night waters across to reach
the distant shore, the white place,
Mictlan, place of souls at rest, place

of blank peace, and place you seek,
meaningful place. She is Xeritzin,
mother of sterile and fertile birth,
she speaks the dead's language, takes

my hand and leads to island
terminus to the path that parts
black waves and points to
white land, the northern land.

The causeway fades off far
ahead into blind night
the only sounds, our feet, the waves,
her bare feet kick up bits of bone

that the spine of dirt holds,
she runs to long wave sounds,
to sorrows unlike petals but greater
perdition, till we reach path's end,

gray flags mark the final exit,
a pale dog waits for us
at causeway end and gray
land extends beyond.

Xeritzin motions me still,
removes black huipil and gently covers
the pale dog's head, she motions
that I follow her past,

off the sorrowful path and forward.
In the graying light I see
her back, skin covered in
cipher of cihuatl, an image

of childbirth I make out
as light transforms a lighter gray,
and then in the distance, white

13 White

Mictlan

Light envelopes Xeritzin, me,
earth tones transform lighter
ahead our every step,
all there reflects all there,

all the long and short of wave
earth glow before us,
sky is fog, fog billows here,
there, and clean brilliant

light in holes between,
for it is a northern land
place of undifferentiated spectrum,
place of bright peace.

My guide points out the souls
at rest who neither see us nor care
as we walk among them, some
reveal faces as if in dream,

others stare at blank codices
as if only to comprehend.
She speaks to one, to others,
their blank eyes blank,

in a language I have never heard,
yet as we walk further white,
the words become intelligible,
bit by bit I learn the concerns

of a young man, and blush in shame
at the words of an old woman.
We press on, the ground becomes sand
like sand in Tulum, and the air,

transparent except where white.
More steps, more souls and we come
to the tlamatini, and beyond, the poet.

Aristotle

The first point, ¿is it? regards
the matter of the real, for what
am I here, but image of my other
self, in this final place, Mictlan,

yes, where all are hard image
against a pervading white
except for questioning poets,
like yourself, and their guides, Xeritzin

here, Virgil, yet if the primary
regards the real, is the first look
a look upon illusory reality
as your paper songs say, mere

shadows cast by infernal glare?
Yes, and further, the site of such
real comes to mean only by
the arc of poets, your acts,

here in this place, Mictlan means true
reflection fashioned in your words,
by the flowers you sing of dead past,
yes, but how can the first point

be fashioned of itself indivisible,
being just self and nothing more,
singularly, but point one? an identity
of self reflection, point one before

the first number, the double, and before one
there can be nothing absent, each point,
part of line, bit of cube, is whole,
yes, a hole, and so a full zero

completes itself, no, no thing
absent, so the image shadow
soul motioning in a white field,
point one, is the identity of self

which cannot be hole because otherwise
impossible? each soul is hole, yet
only known by living poesis or the gods,
but here, is mere white reflection

of that, and yet truly, Equis,
tlahcuiloco of floricanto, as well
as Gato and Xeritzin and all other
souls alive, live only in the inks,

in the red and the black, for only in
codices do bodies truly animate,
do you imagine the incidents of death,
your father, my teacher's teacher,

are held only there? are a line
of events only in relation,
only incidents of history?
know this, you come to life

in the cantos I sing, your acts
your body, so many petals lying
on white sand, gain color
but not fact, in the poems, your line,

its cross, and the points it divides
are simple fact and not true,
for it is the flower and the song
that marks the sole zero,

that marks difference, not one.

Marie Uguay

Xeritzin takes me from the Tlamatini
leads to where white sand
stops cold, to where white heaps
snow cold below dunes

of cold fog spill one last exit,
to where there in the snow,
the face of a woman lies
perfect face, this poet,

dark hair, pale lips and a white skin
lost in snow. Xeritzin
kneels and lets red hair drape
over the cold face and across,

presses her lips to hers,
the eyes open, the face
speaks to my guide of me,
son corps est un point fixe,

but here in Mictlan, life beyond,
she gathers petals from three rivers
for song and sings to me
je vous porte dans vos silences historiques,

beyond the whole wave the dead
and real, bercé revêtue
par la blancheur infernale du jour,
the frozen coordinates of flame

and the true, and yet I pause
before the perfect face
and ask if she is probable,
not fact, but true, and if her breath

is bright fog or verbal reflection
of codex ink, and Xeritzin's
body marks, a floricanto
of life beyond. She whispers

in my ear, Xeritzin exhales
fog and steps back, back
in the brilliant white, and I
cup snow in my own hands and cover

the perfect face.

3/3:

california no
es isla

14   Polylogue

One Site, Two Souls, Hour Zero

Peninsula-tepic
Lola Arc and other poet
l'outre-heure

Δ

Hill at peninsula end point
inscribed by water, a vapor air,
she, cool northern light,
he follows fault lines where
time can only describe
hour dreams and impossible daze

Δ

Pacific, gulf and bay
define la Isla California,
Cabos to Saint Francis,
where Lola moves in words and dance
mnemotechny, he draws ink
live action, prepares to imagine
lines of imaginary syntax without
ordinal syntactic corps, for no first word
is made from zero night mimesis

Δ

The north peninsular extreme, so altern,
red bridge instead of rock arch,
the ocean ends inland and white
fog spills white all summer white,
Lola refuses change back to fleshless
philosopher's daughter, still she runs tidal sand,
and graciously he accepts water, the fluid held by hyper-
cooled fluid, he speaks and hears, and why not?
speech is enabled by shifting proximities even if empty
of any real river of hours, hearing, even if distance and spin
made sense without linear desire and transformation
meant locus and point and motion.

Δ

This site, meters uphill, breathes hard,
vantage point at bay, 122 by 37, context of particular
earth and sky and sea and fog in motion
circumscribes her face and perfect word, she imagines
vanilla orchids, he, a hummingbird, perfectly
hover, still, unbelievably quick,
a flap in no time change merely beside the
smaller distance of flower and changes all at altern
angles, altern light from holes in opaque night

Δ

City of streets, landfill full of abandoned ships,
singular arc of one sole sun
illuminate ciphers she shapes by moving hand
as well as the font he imagines full
not at the moment, instance without instants,
full motion across dead time, pale of history

Δ

Peninsular cityscape points in sky
where she lives, he reflects
lost continuity, contiguous typeface

15   Ordinal Syntax

This angle of sun, phase of moon,
gluon proximate quark
can never will be
can never were,
but for a taut tense schema,
grapheme and phoneme,
red and at times harmonious,
that relates artist line to human form,
lyric, to mito doloroso
its grammar but orders beyond life
never life.

Imagine a man with fingertip stained ink
draws the Virgen de Guadalupe
he wants sacred, her face is perfect, radiates,
but the stain nags, random,
intimate, blood red or blood black
not part of the arc drawing, perhaps
erase the mark under rapture
or conceive all reality lies in it only?
or peel back skin tomorrow or not take up pen
hours ago as the taut tense makes real?
One absent flowers does not exist, nor
its virtual progeny, and here
this live conjunction is already dead.

16 Vida Nueva

Font is not
the perfect typeface
but metonym that holds
the perfect frøzen accident
that resounds and shines
any place I go

Some there she holds me
by the margins, gathers
petals and leaves
changes her red heart,
radiates yellow,
holds black thorns
against a white snow

of childhood I make out
as light transforms a lighter gray
and then in the distance when